GASLIGHTED
GASLIGHT 1944 AND 2020

YOU ARE BEING GASLIGHTED

Compiled and Edited

By

David L. Brown, Ph.D.

Copyright © 2020 by Dr. David L. Brown
All Rights Reserved
Printed in the United States of America

ISBN 978-1-7356723-1-1

All Scripture quotes are from the King James Bible.

No part of this work may be reproduced without the expressed consent of the publisher, except for brief quotes, whether by electronic, photocopying, recording, or information storage and retrieval systems.

Address All Inquiries To:
THE OLD PATHS PUBLICATIONS, Inc.
142 Gold Flume Way
Cleveland, Georgia, U.S.A. 30528

Web: www.theoldpathspublications.com
E-mail: TOP@theoldpathspublications.com

TABLE OF CONTENTS

- TABLE OF CONTENTS 3
- CHRISTIANS BE AWARE OF WHAT IS GOING ON! 4
- WHO IS THE AUTHOR AND ADVOCATE FOR LYING?. 6
- WHAT IS GASLIGHTING? 7
- A PERPETUAL STATE OF GASLIGHTING 8
- THE BIBLICAL FAMILY STRUCTURE 9
- POLICE ARE A THREAT? 10
- THE ASSAULT ON CAPITALISM 12
- WHITE FRAGILITY 13
- THE MEDIA'S TOP LIES & SPINS ABOUT COVID-19 17
- PRESIDENT TRUMP IS THEIR FAVORITE TARGET, AS THESE EXAMPLES SHOW. 17
- WHAT KIND OF A CHRISTIAN ARE YOU? 26
- ABOUT THE AUTHOR 28
- SOME OF HIS OTHER PUBLICATIONS INCLUDE: 30

I am appalled at the politicians and news media that spew lies! Paul H. Weaver, in his provocative analysis entitled *News and the Culture of Lying: How Journalism Really Works* said, "Journalists and politicians have become ensnared in a symbiotic [mutual beneficial relationship between two groups] web of lies that mislead the public." He wrote that 26 years ago but it has grown to deadly proportions today! True journalism...reporting the facts is virtually dead! Today they write from a set of skewed values. They have no interest in the truth.

As I see it, **Isaiah 59:14** describes the day we are living in.

> *"Judgment is turned away backward, and justice standeth afar off: for truth is fallen in the street, and equity cannot enter."*

CHRISTIANS BE AWARE OF WHAT IS GOING ON!

Ephesians 4:14 says,

> *"That we henceforth be no more children, tossed to and fro, and carried about with every wind of doctrine, by the sleight of men,*

and cunning craftiness, whereby **they lie in wait to deceive**."

There are seven things that God hates and which are an abomination to Him. We read of them in

Proverbs 6:16-19

> "These six things doth the LORD hate: yea, seven are an abomination unto him: 17 A proud look, **a lying tongue**, and hands that shed innocent blood, 18 An heart that deviseth wicked imaginations, feet that be swift in running to mischief, 19 **A false witness that speaketh lies**, and he that soweth discord among brethren."

Proverbs 12:22

> "Lying lips are abomination to the LORD: but they that deal truly are his delight."

Proverbs 14:5

> "A faithful witness will not lie: but a false witness will utter lies."

WHO IS THE AUTHOR AND ADVOCATE FOR LYING?

In Christ's day it was the Pharisees, who were trying to control the narrative. But who empowered them?

John 8:44-45

> "Ye are of your father the devil, and the lusts of your father ye will do. He was a murderer from the beginning, and <u>abode not in the truth, because there is no truth in him</u>. When he speaketh a lie, he speaketh of his own: for <u>he is a liar</u>, and <u>the father of it</u>. 45 And because I tell you the truth, ye believe me not."

My Christian friends, we are living in a day of national apostasy where reality is being turned upside-down much like it was in Isaiah's day –

Isaiah 5:20 & 23

> "Woe unto them that call evil good, and good evil; that put darkness for light, and light for darkness; that put bitter for sweet, and sweet for bitter! 23

GASLIGHTED

> *Which justify the wicked for reward, and take away the righteousness of the righteous from him!"*

What is the outworking of this replacing evil for good today? I suggest that **we are being Gaslighted**! I have heard this term several times in political rhetoric and wondered what it meant.

WHAT IS GASLIGHTING?

"Gaslighting" is used to describe abusive behavior, specifically when an **abuser manipulates information in such a way as to make a victim question his or her sanity.** Gaslighting intentionally makes someone doubt their memories or perception of reality.

The term Gaslighting originates in the systematic psychological manipulation of a victim by her husband in Patrick Hamilton's 1938 stage play **Gaslight**, and the film adaptations released in 1940 and 1944. In the story, the husband attempts to convince his wife and others that she is insane by manipulating small elements of their environment and insisting that she is mistaken, remembering things incorrectly, or delusional when she points out these changes. The play's title alludes to how the abusive husband slowly dims the gas lights in their home, while pretending nothing has changed, in an effort to make his wife doubt her own perceptions. The wife repeatedly asks her husband to confirm her perceptions about the dimming lights, but in defiance of reality, he keeps insisting that the lights are the same and instead it is she who is going insane.

A PERPETUAL STATE OF GASLIGHTING

My question is, are we, as a nation, being gaslighted? In fact WE ARE! We are living in **a perpetual state of gaslighting**. The left is attempting to "alter reality" by pushing a false narrative in an effort to convince as many Americans as possible that their view is the only sensible, reasonable view and if you hold a different view you are an extremist, and something is wrong with you!

The alleged "reality" that is being peddled by the media is at complete odds with what we are seeing with our own two eyes. And when we question the false reality (fake news) that we are being presented, or we claim that what we see is that actual reality, <u>we are vilified as racist or bigots or just plain crazy.</u> You're not racist. You're not crazy. **You're being gaslighted**.

Let's look at some false claims that are being presented by the technique of *gaslighting*.

THE BIBLICAL FAMILY STRUCTURE

Also called the nuclear family, with a male father and female mother united in marriage and seeking to rear children, has been the backbone of society ever since the creation of man and woman. However, if you believe in this structure, with the father as the head, the media and the left attack you as being sexist, racist, fascist, etc. They claim this is a white social structure. You are called a gay-hating bigot. Belief in the nuclear family is terribly bad for society and must be destroyed. This is an example of *gaslighting*.

There is a hidden motive behind the political left's attacking of the social structure of the family, which explains why the political left just despises it, calling it "patriarchal" and "fascist," and work to destroy it. If you take away the family structure, <u>people will be forced to become more reliant on the state for those things they previously received from</u>

their families, thus allowing the state more control of their lives. It's just another step closer to the left's ultimate goal of having a government that has complete control over our lives and bring in Socialism. In reality this is the very definition of fascism – which is authoritarian ultranationalism characterized by dictatorial power, forcible suppression of opposition, as well as strong regimentation of society and of the economy.

POLICE ARE A THREAT?

Another claim is Police are a threat to law and order, and especially terrible for the black community. We see the major problem destroying many inner-cities is crime; murder, gang violence, drug dealing, drive-by shootings and armed robbery, but we are told that it is not crime, but the police that are the problem in the inner-cities. We are told we must defund the police and remove law enforcement from crime-riddled cities to make them safer. If you believe that, **you've been gaslighted**.

Less police presence does NOT make things safer as we see in Portland, Seattle, Chicago and New York City. In fact, just 22 miles from

GASLIGHTED

my house, a black man was shot while committing a crime and I saw mobs of people looting stores, smashing windows, setting cars on fire and burning down buildings, but we are told that these demonstrations are mostly peaceful protests. And when we call this destruction of our cities riots, <u>we are called racists</u>. So, we ask ourselves, am I crazy? No, **you're being gaslighted**.

The catastrophe is the *Black Lives Matter* movement has caused the police to back off, emboldening the violent members of the black community, thus causing violent crimes and homicides to skyrocket out of control. <u>The *Black Lives Matter* movement has literally caused tens of thousands of black lives to not matter</u>. **But if we advocate for more policing in cities overrun by crime, we are accused of being white supremacists and racists**. It should be noted that one of the founders of Black Lives Matter admitted involvement in Occultism and Divination at one of the Centers of BLM.
(www.worldviewweekend.com/tv/video/founder-black-lives-matter-admits-occultism-divination-center-blm)

Yep, that's practically what they're doing...

GASLIGHTED

So, we ask ourselves, am I crazy? No, **you're being gaslighted**.

Yet another illustration of **gaslighting** is that **we need completely open borders and let everyone that wants to come in with no vetting.** The United States of America accepts more immigrants than any other country in the world. The vast majority of the immigrants are "people of color," and these immigrants are enjoying freedom and economic opportunity not available to them in their country of origin, but <u>we are told that the United States is the most racist and oppressive country on the planet</u>, and <u>if we disagree, we are called racist and xenophobic</u>. Advocating having a vetting process so we keep out criminals and terrorists, and controlling the number of immigrants so we aren't overwhelmed, and not having open borders, does not make someone xenophobic and anti-immigrant. But the left's political rhetoric wants you to believe you are uncaring and crazy. Their real goal is once again to collapse the system, and that is not good for anyone. So, we ask ourselves, am I crazy? No, **you're being gaslighted**.

THE ASSAULT ON CAPITALISM

Then there is **the assault on Capitalism and the push for Socialism.** Capitalist countries are the most prosperous countries in the world. The standard of living is the highest in capitalist countries. We see more poor people move up the economic ladder to the middle and even the wealthy class through their effort and ability in capitalist countries than any other economic system in the world, but we are told capitalism is an oppressive system designed to keep people down. So, we ask ourselves, am I crazy? **No, you're being gaslighted**.

Communist countries killed over 100 million people in the 20th century. Communist countries strip their citizens of basic human rights, dictate every aspect of their lives, treat their citizens like slaves, and drive their economies into the ground, but we are told that Communism is the fairest, most equitable, freest and most prosperous economic system in the world. So, we ask ourselves, am I crazy? **No, you're being gaslighted**.

WHITE FRAGILITY

One of the most egregious examples of gaslighting is the concept of "**white fragility**". You spend your life trying to be a good person, trying to treat people fairly and with respect. You disavow racism and bigotry in all its forms. You judge people solely on the content of their character and not by the color of their skin. You don't discriminate based on race or ethnicity. But you are told you are a racist, not because of something you did or said, but solely because of the color of your skin. If you do not affirm Black Lives Matter, but rather believe that All Lives Matter you are a racist and a white supremacist. You know instinctively that charging someone with racism because of their skin color is itself racist. You know that you are not racist, so you defend yourself and your character, but you are told that your defense of yourself is proof of your racism. So, we ask ourselves, am I crazy? No, **you're being gaslighted**.

Gaslighting has become one of the most pervasive and destructive tactics in American politics. It is the exact opposite of what our political system was meant to be. It deals in lies and psychological coercion, and not truth and intellectual discourse. If you ever ask yourself if you're crazy, you are not. Crazy people aren't sane enough to ask themselves if they're crazy. So, remember what the Bible says:

Isaiah 5:20& 23

> *"Woe unto them that call evil good, and good evil; that put darkness for light, and light for*

darkness; that put bitter for sweet, and sweet for bitter! 23 Which justify the wicked for reward, and take away the righteousness of the righteous from him!"

Right is right, wrong is wrong and wrong is sin! Trust your eyes over what you are told. Never listen to the people who tell you that you are crazy, because you are not, **you're being gaslighted.**

Nazi Propaganda Minister Joseph Goebbels, who was called the Poison Dwarf, said, "If you tell a lie big enough and keep repeating it, people will eventually come to believe it. The lie can be maintained only for such time as the State can shield the people from the political, economic and/or military consequences of the lie. It thus becomes vitally important for the State to use all of its powers to repress dissent, for the truth is the mortal enemy of the lie, and thus by extension, the truth is the greatest enemy of the State."

The left and the media are doing all they can to gaslight us. The Cancel Culture is all about telling and repeating BIG LIES in a desperate effort to get people to believe them and keep the truth from being known and believed.

Sophocles said: "What people believe prevails over the truth."

Proverbs 12:17

> *"He that speaketh truth sheweth forth righteousness: but a false witness deceit."*

1 Thessalonians 5:21

> *"Prove all things; hold fast that which is good."*

Resources

https://bloomp.net/articles/guide-to-the-political-lefts-attempts-at-altering-reality-through-gaslighting.htm

www.realclearpolitics.com/articles/2020/03/29/the_medias_top_lies_and_spins_about_covid-19.html

www.worldviewweekend.com/tv/video/founder-black-lives-matter-admits-occultism-divination-center-blm

https://www.washingtonexaminer.com/opinion/black-lives-matter-is-posing-a-legitimate-safety-threat-and-its-not-racist-to-point-that-out

THE MEDIA'S TOP LIES AND SPINS ABOUT COVID-19

I found this sight to be very telling. The title of the article is: *The Media's Top Lies and Spins About COVID-19* (www.realclearpolitics.com/articles/2020/03/29/the_medias_top_lies_and_spins_about_covid-19.html)

The media distorts and misleads, takes statements out of context, treats assumptions as facts, and in general, seems to want to sow as much rancor and fear as possible. This is irresponsible journalism in a time when the nation needs just the opposite.

PRESIDENT TRUMP IS THEIR FAVORITE TARGET, AS THESE EXAMPLES SHOW.

- **February 28, 2020:** Politico published a piece entitled, "Trump rallies his base to treat coronavirus as a 'hoax.'" Many in the media and Democratic Party echoed this fake news. Trump was in fact calling the criticisms of his administration's response to the coronavirus the Democrats' new hoax.
- **March 5, 2020:** CBS News posted a story falsely claiming President Trump told sick people to go to work. If you read the actual quote, he is talking about healthy people going about their

business not knowing that they have the virus: "So if, you know, we have thousands or hundreds of thousands of people that get better, just by, you know, sitting around and even going to work, some of them go to work, but they get better."

- **March 12, 2020**: An Atlantic staff writer upheld the lie that China was "sending aid" to Italy out of goodwill, despite it being disproven by The Washington Post. The shipments in question were exports that had been purchased by Italy and other receiving countries.
- **March 12, 2020**: NBC, NPR, Newsweek, Joe Biden, CNN, and Esquire falsely claimed that President Trump blocked coronavirus testing and rejected WHO coronavirus test kits because lower numbers are good for his re-election.
- **March 13, 2020**: The stock market soared and the Dow Jones Industrial Average closed at a record increase after President Trump and his coronavirus task force held a press conference on the government's response. CNN had only criticisms of the administration's response with no mention of the stock market gains, according to The Federalist.

- **March 13, 2020**: The Washington Post published an opinion piece that falsely claimed that President Trump closed the White House Pandemic Office. The Washington Post later released an article that fact checked the initial claims from the opinion piece.
- **March 15, 2020.** The Atlantic published a piece, "The Coronavirus Called America's Bluff," that attempted to assert the Trump administration is just as bad as China's Communist Party in its handling of the coronavirus. Keep in mind that China silenced doctors and journalists and lied to the WHO to keep the pandemic under wraps.
- **March 16, 2020:** The Daily Beast took a cheap shot at the president, but worse, it misled Americans when it headlined a story, "President Trump told several governors that they are largely on their own in stocking up on gear such as respirators and ventilators to fight the novel coronavirus." Other outlets then echoed the phony report. The president actually said, "We will be backing you, but try getting it yourselves. Point of sales, much better, much more direct if you can get it yourself."

- **March 16, 2020**: CNN falsely claimed that the Trump administration is considering imposing a national curfew.
- **March 16, 2020**: Reuters, The Guardian, Business Insider, and staffers at the New York Times and MSNBC falsely claim that Trump wants to monopolize a coronavirus vaccine.
- **March 17, 2020:** In a tweet, MSNBC analyst Glenn Kirschner suggests Donald Trump is guilty of negligent homicide "for the way he's mishandled the Coronavirus crisis."
- **March 17, 2020:** A doctored tweet suggesting that President Trump would withhold federal aid from his critics circulates on Twitter and Instagram, which FactCheck.org debunked.
- **March 18, 2020:** A Washington Post columnist falsely accused Senate Majority Leader Mitch McConnell of delaying the House's vote on the coronavirus bill. (To its credit, the paper later ran a correction at the top of the column.)
- **March 18, 2020:** Rick Wilson tweets "#BeInfected" in response to a story about First Lady Melania Trump appearing in public health PSA's on the coronavirus, which he later said was a joke, deriding the First Lady's #BeBest campaign.

- **March 19, 2020**: NBC News published a story entitled, "Italy has a world class health system. The coronavirus has pushed it to the breaking point." Despite NBC's best efforts to fear monger, a quick Google search tells us that Johns Hopkins ranks Italy's system, in relation to treating the sick and protecting health care workers, as number 54 in the world.
- **March 20, 2020**: The Daily Mail criticized Trump for calling the coronavirus the Chinese virus, dubbing it racist when the outlet itself used the term just two short months ago because the virus did, indeed, originate in China.
- **March 20, 2020:** CNN published a story entitled, "Yes, Of Course Donald Trump Is Calling Coronavirus The 'China Virus' For Political Reasons."
- **March 20, 2020:** The Atlantic published a piece blaming President Trump's personality for the coronavirus outbreak.
- **March 22, 2020:** The New York Times changed a headline from, "Democrats Block Action on $1.8 Trillion Stimulus" to one that blames "partisan divide."
- **March 23, 2020:** Morning Joe host Joe Scarborough tweeted: "There is no public benefit to this briefing. The

networks should all cut away." This tweet came despite recent polling that shows the majority of Americans approve of President Trump's response to the coronavirus and disapprove of the media's coverage.

- **March 23, 2020**: A tabloid run by the Communist Party of China posted a video that contained footage of American media outlets and politicians repeating China's talking points to portray China's response to the coronavirus as favorable.
- **March 23, 2020:** An NBC Reporter insinuated that President Trump is responsible for the death of a man who consumed fish tank cleaner. You must read further into her thread to get the crucial fact — that what the man consumed was a parasite treatment for fish, not the medical form of Chloroquine that President Trump has discussed. It's worth noting the salacious tweet alleging President Trump's responsibility in this received over 34k retweets, while the final tweet in the thread specifying that the toxic ingredient consumed by the man was not actually the medical form of the drug in question got fewer than 3k retweets.

- **March 24, 2020**: MSNBC host Rachel Maddow tweeted that cable news networks should stop covering the President's coronavirus briefings, propagating that the President is amplifying misinformation. Seattle NPR announced they will stop airing the President's coronavirus briefings. Coincidentally, networks are wanting to cut coverage of these briefings as President Trump's approval rating hits its highest level since 2017.
- **March 26, 2020**: Vox published a story "Trump's reckless promotion of hydroxychloroquine to fight coronavirus, explained." Vox failed to mention that when Anthony Fauci was asked if he would prescribe hydroxychloroquine he said "Yeah, of course, particularly if people have no other option. These drugs are approved drugs for other reasons."

In January of this year, the Trump administration took definitive action to slow the spread of the contagion by placing travel restrictions on China. The administration received harsh criticism in the press for this decision; Politico even wrote a story citing public health experts who feared that the Trump administration's aggressive response could backfire.

Since then, the Trump administration has declared a national emergency, allowing states to access over $42 billion in existing funding. President Trump signed the Families First Coronavirus Response Act, ensuring that American families and businesses impacted by the virus receive the support that they need. President Trump has expanded testing accessibility and is supporting American families, workers, and small businesses with aid and other programs. The president is taking all necessary measures and cutting red tape to support patients and health care providers while working to replenish essential medical supplies and promote the development of a vaccine.

While President Trump and his team are working together to bring hope, safety, financial relief, and a vaccine to Americans, the press has been busy promoting its own politicized narrative of the coronavirus. Sadly for the media, the majority of Americans approve of President Trump's response to the coronavirus. The daily efforts by the administration to inform the public of developments have toppled the sensational, politicized narrative of the press. This is a perfect example of how strong executive leadership can ease the fear of a nation in times of crisis. Another job well done, President Trump.

Cora Mandy is a spokeswoman for America First Action, an organization in support of the Trump administration.

WHAT KIND OF A CHRISTIAN ARE YOU?

There are differing views among Americans as to how a person becomes a Christian. I find that there are three main categories:
>Man-made Christians
>Self-made Christians
>God-made Christians

Man-made Christians base their view of Christianity upon what others have said, especially their spiritual leader. They believe they are a real Christian because they were told, taught or it was implied that they were Christians for whatever reason, be it baptism, religious activities, keeping religious traditions, etc. That is *false!* True Christianity is based upon what the Bible says, *We ought to obey God rather than men.* Acts 5:29

Self-made Christians think they are accepted by God because of all the good things they have done. They are often good moral people, actively involved in church, doing their best to earn their salvation by their good works. That is *false!* The Bible says, *For by grace are ye saved through faith; and that not of yourselves: it is the gift of God, Not of works, lest any man should boast.* Ephesians 2:8-9

God-made Christians are the only real Christians. A person must become a Christian God's way! The Bible clearly points out that God has a plan for our salvation. *And we have seen and do testify that the Father sent the Son to be the Savior of the world. (I John 4:14) For God so loved the world, that he gave his only begotten Son, that whosoever believeth in him should not perish, but have everlasting life. (John 3:16)*

RECEIVE JESUS CHRIST TO BE A REAL CHRISTIAN – *Believe on the Lord Jesus Christ, and thou shalt be saved.* Acts 16:31

ADMIT YOU ARE A SINNER – *For all have sinned, and come short of the glory of God;* Romans 3:23

REALIZE THAT SALVATION FROM SIN IS A GIFT – *For the wages of sin is death; but the gift of God is eternal life through Jesus Christ our Lord.* Romans 6:23

BELIEVE THAT CHRIST DIED FOR YOUR SINS & AROSE FROM THE DEAD – *That if thou shalt confess with thy mouth the Lord Jesus, and shalt believe in thine heart that God hath raised him from the dead, thou shalt be saved.* Romans 10:9

BELIEVE THAT CHRIST IS THE ONLY WAY OF SALVATION – *Jesus saith unto him, I am the way, the truth, and the life: no man cometh unto the Father, but by me.* John 14:6

PRAY AND ASK CHRIST TO FORGIVE YOUR SINS AND SAVE YOUR SOUL – *For whosoever shall call upon the name of the Lord shall be saved.* Romans 10:13

ABOUT THE AUTHOR

David L. Brown was born in Michigan. He came to know Christ as his Savior as the result of a Sunday  school teacher throwing away the liberal curriculum, teaching through the book of Romans, and sharing the Gospel. He has been married to Linda for 49 years. She was a young lady from his home church.

David attended a Michigan University then transferred to a Christian University and Seminary where he completed a Bachelor's Degree in Social Science and Theology. He holds a Master's Degree in Theology, and Ph.D. in History, specializing in the history of the English Bible.

Since December 1979, he has been the Pastor of the First Baptist Church of Oak Creek, Wisconsin (an independent, fundamental, Baptist Church using the King James Bible and conservative music). Previous to that, he pastored an independent Baptist Church in Michigan for five years, was an assistant pastor for 4 years, and served with his wife as short-term missionaries in Haiti.

Dr. Brown is the president of the **King James Bible Research Council**:

(www.kjbresearchcouncil.com), an organization dedicated to promoting the King James Bible and its underlying texts and other traditional text translations around the world in a solid and sensible way.

He is also the president of **Logos Communication Consortium, Inc.** (www.logosresourcepages.org), a research organization that produces a large variety of materials warning Christians of present dangers in our culture. He is also the vice president of the **Midwest Independent Baptist Pastor's Fellowship**, a fellowship of independent Baptist pastors, missionaries, and evangelists from fourteen upper Midwest states.

Dr. Brown is the Curator of the **Christian Heritage Bible Collection** and regularly takes his rare Bible, manuscript and artifact collection to fundamental Baptist Churches teaching and preaching on the history of our English Bible, showing how God has preserved His Word(s), and why we should use the King James Bible.

He also serves as a consultant for individuals, museums, colleges, universities, and seminaries that desire to acquire or have collections of biblical manuscripts and Bibles. He is an antiquarian book dealer with contacts around the world.

SOME OF HIS OTHER PUBLICATIONS INCLUDE:

1. *The Indestructible Book,* a 500 page, hardback with a cover
2. *The Indestructible Book, a 500 page, perfect bound book*
3. *God's Blueprint For Marriage & Family*, a perfect bound book, 108 pages
4. *The Defined Geneva Bible, New Testament, With Modern Spelling*, Editor, hardback, 344 pages
5. *The Geneva Bible, Old Testament, With Modern Spelling,* Editor, hardback, 970 pages.
6. *The Dark Side of Halloween*
7. *The 1576 Tyndale New Testament and Biography*, Hardback, 540 pages, Editor
8. Editor - *The Bible Source Book*

He can be contacted at:

Dr. David L. Brown
8044 S. Verdev Dr.
Oak Creek, WI. 53154
Phone: 414-768-9754
Email: PastorDavidLBrown@gmail.com

www.ingramcontent.com/pod-product-compliance
Lightning Source LLC
Chambersburg PA
CBHW061316040426
42444CB00010B/2670